The Echo's

THIRD 1

G000254636

Cotswold

Walks

by Christopher Knowles

Ten more walks compiled from the Lifestyle supplement of the
Gloucestershire Echo.

Family strolls of between 2 and 5 miles, including refreshment
stops along the way.

REARDON & SON
Cheltenham, England

INDEX

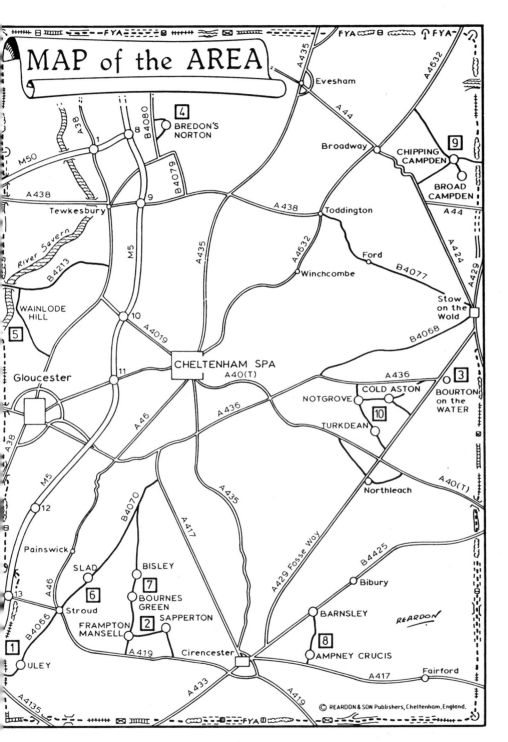

MAP of the AREA

1 Uley Bury

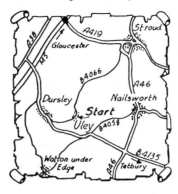

Distance: 2¹/₂ miles
Time: 1¹/₂ hours of continuous walking
Map: OS Pathfinder 1132 (ST 69/79 Dursley and Wotton-Under-Edge)
Starting Point: Grid ref 789984
Terrain: A little road, but mostly grassy path with a considerable climb at the beginning.
Refreshments: The Old Crown at Uley.

This walk keeps us towards the southern part of the Cotswolds but perhaps a little beyond our usual boundaries. It is, furthermore, rather shorter than some, but ideal for a warm summer's day or a more gentle stroll.

Uley is a pretty village at the far end of the Cam valley which straggles quite steeply down Frocester Hill to a green, a church, an old-fashioned petrol station and a good pub. South of the green is a post office and you should try to park in its vicinity.

Uley owes much of its former importance and subsequent prosperity to its development as a cloth village just preceding the Industrial Revolution, famous in particular for the production of blue cloth – many of its houses therefore date back to the 18th century. It was during the Napoleonic wars that the population rose dramatically as demand for cloth for the army soared (although it has also been said that cloth here was made for the French too). In 1827 a local man, Edward Sheppard, was one of the first to import Merino wool from Australia.

Curiously for a village of such importance a school was not founded here at this time. The river here, from which Uley developed as a cloth centre, is the Ewelme, which joins the Severn near Frampton. The church, in keeping with the village's industrial heritage, is Victorian.

Just to the right of the post office (as you look at it) is a narrow tarmac lane. Follow this as it ascends gently between some houses before reverting to a track. At its end you will see a gate and a stile leading into a steep meadow; but on the right, immediately preceding it, is a gateway leading into an area of sheds, greenhouses and garden plots. Immediately before the gateway, also on the right, is an easily-overlooked pathway.

Turn into this and follow it as it passes through a tunnel of green, passing wooden fencing on the right, behind which is the anonymous roof of a house, with the occasional glimpse of the church ahead of you to the right. The path rises slightly before you arrive at the churchyard beyond a stone wall to the right, but very soon after this a narrow path appears on the left.

Take this as it ascends a little more steeply between hedges and through overhanging nettles and grasses, passing a cottage on the left to finally come to a halt at a kissing gate on the edge of a meadow.

Go through the gate to find yourself confronted by a steep slope rising over a little ridge to woodland, and sweeping broadly to left and right. You need to go straight up towards the trees, keeping fractionally to the left; but a stop is recommended as you climb through meadow flowers, not merely to rest but also to enjoy the eminently satisfying views that open up behind you, across the roofs of Uley to Owlpen Manor on the right (distinguishable by the trees which surround it, growing out of a patch of emerald green) and the tree-laden slopes on the other side of the valley. The Manor is partly medieval and is said to have once welcomed Margaret of Anjou, Henry VI's queen, on her way to the Battle of Tewkesbury in 1470. She is supposed to haunt the manor, as indeed is the Black Monk, who apparently starved to death here as he fled the sack of Kingswood Abbey.

At the tree line, where the woods recede up the hill slightly, you need to look for a bridle gate. Go through this onto a woodland path which threads its way through a sea of cool, slender trees swaying gently like kelp on the tide. The path continues to climb fairly obviously along a miniature escarpment with a deeper, wider path below to the left.

After some time you will come to a wire fence at which point you should follow the path as it veers left, with the fence on the right. Then the path comes to an end at a stile. Cross this and continue the ascent straight ahead, ignoring paths coming in from the left and right. Soon, as you catch sight of hillocks and hummocks ahead, you will emerge into the open air and climb through wild grasses to another fence, where a substantial path goes left and right across the ridge.

Turn right and follow this path which is like a gutter on the edge of a roof with the roof to the left and a severe drop below you to the right, towards the fields of Uley. This windswept path, neatly following the contours of the hill, will bring you ultimately to a row of posts and then a clearing, at the end of which is a pole lying horizontally across the ground. Go over or around this and then immediately to the left, to follow the path as it continues along the lip of the hill.

Within seconds a gap between the bushes opens up to the right to reveal a view of startling beauty across the slim fields of the vale to Cambridge, Slimbridge, Berkeley Castle perhaps, the River Severn and the Forest of Dean. As always such views in the Cotswolds are of a magnificence which astounds, seemingly belonging to an altogether different scale for, after all, the height above sea level here is only about 600 feet.

The path continues along the edge and the views to the right come and go whilst the ridge on the left gives no clue as to what lies behind. This is Uley Bury, once upon a time an animal stockade (and indeed the smell of horse still comes at you on the breeze) as well as a Iron Age promontory fort dating from the last centuries BC of which it is considered one of the finest examples in the country. It covers an area of 30 acres and would have sheltered up to 2000 people.

Follow the path as it rounds along the edge of the fort until another corner (ignoring a yellow arrow and a stile which invite you to descend to the right off the main track) after which the rampart to the left lowers to reveal cultivated land.

Continue once again, with a sheer drop beneath you to the right and a view, to a curiously regular hill crowned with a row of trees. Beyond is the village of Dursley and in the distance the William Tyndale monument, stark to the sky. Eventually you will come to the next, southeast, corner where Uley can be espied below you once again and where there is a little hummock to the right. Take a path over this and begin to descend fairly steeply through the undergrowth, with Owlpen Manor now

5

somewhat closer than before.

Not long after there will be a choice of paths at which point you should take the left fork. Several other paths will lure you away as you go down but ignore them, and any yellow arrows, and keep to the main, crumbly path for quite some time as it descends into undergrowth. After this steepish descent you will arrive at a stile at the edge of a field.

At the right hand margin of the field is a tarmac path. Follow this down as it passes a small power station and then an orchard garden to the right, with views to the church and slope you climbed earlier to the left. The path curves to the left to skirt a white cottage and then fetches up at a stile on the right.

Go over the stile and pass in front of the cottage until you come to a narrow traffic lane. Turn left here and follow it down past a fine stone wall and pretty gardens towards the main road. As you approach this you will pass the famous Uley 'Old Spot' brewery on the left. At the road turn left onto the pavement and follow the road up through Uley village, with its grey stone houses, until you return to the post office.

The sketch shows the entrance to Uley Long Barrow, better known as Hetty Pegler's Tump. The mound is over 100 ft long and is about 350 yards north of Uley Bury. The name of Hetty Pegler came from the owner of the land on which the Barrow was situated in the 17th Century.

6

The ULEY BURY Walk

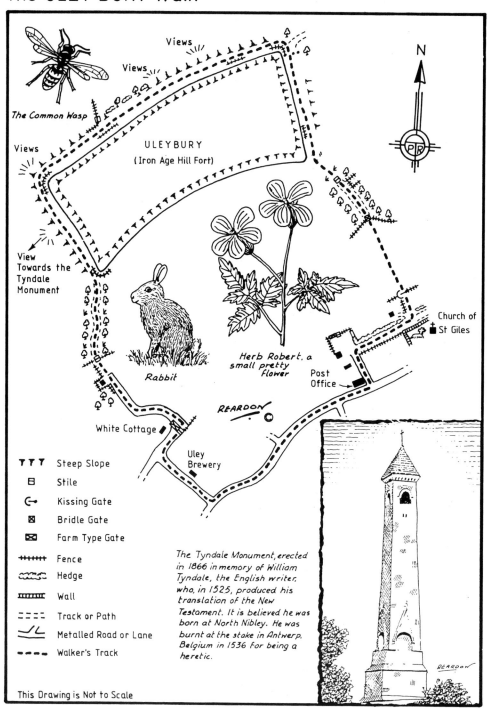

The Common Wasp

Views
Views
Views

ULEYBURY
(Iron Age Hill Fort)

Views

View
Towards the
Tyndale
Monument

N
P T R

Church of
St Giles

Herb Robert, a
small pretty
Flower

Post
Office

Rabbit

REARDON

White Cottage

Uley
Brewery

▼ ▼ ▼	Steep Slope
🅱	Stile
↪	Kissing Gate
⊠	Bridle Gate
⋈	Farm Type Gate
╫╫╫	Fence
ᨖᨖᨖ	Hedge
▥▥▥	Wall
═ ═ ═	Track or Path
⟋⟍	Metalled Road or Lane
▬ ▬ ▬	Walker's Track

The Tyndale Monument, erected
in 1866 in memory of William
Tyndale, the English writer,
who, in 1525, produced his
translation of the New
Testament. It is believed he was
born at North Nibley. He was
burnt at the stake in Antwerp,
Belgium in 1536 for being a
heretic.

REARDON

This Drawing is Not to Scale

2 Sapperton-Frampton Mansell

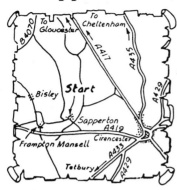

Distance: 3³/₄ miles
Time: 2 hours of continuous walking.
Map: OS Pathfinder 113 (SO 80/90 Stroud)
Starting Point: Grid ref 948034
Terrain: Fields, firm canal towpaths, road and woodland tracks which can be pretty muddy after a lot of rain. Most of the walk is on the flat.
Refreshments: The Bell at Sapperton, the Daneway Inn and the Bell at Frampton Mansell.

Canals round the southern Cotswolds make ideal walking ground, especially on warm days when to walk too far would be strenuous. This area has a very special character, where there is a sense of a failed invasion by the Industrial Revolution.

The starting point in Sapperton is just to the east of the church, along a No Through Road. The church, surrounded by a densely-packed graveyard, is small and picturesque with plants sprouting from its spire which is surmounted by a golden cockerel. The interior is a world of Jacobean carving work, much of which was formerly in a house demolished by Lord Bathurst in 1730, the site of which lies to the north of the church.

There are some fine monuments within, most notably to Sir Henry Poole and to the duellist and county historian, Sir Robert Atkyns. Outside are the graves of Ernest Gimson and the Barnsleys, important figures in the 19th century Arts and Crafts Movement, all of whom lived in Sapperton. Buried here, too, is Rebekah Mason, wife of the astronomer who gave his name to the Mason-Dixon line which divided the southern from the northern states in the pre-Civil War USA.

From here return to the junction by a proper red telephone box and bear right (the pub is to the left). Sapperton, or 'Sapperton's fair dale' as Alexander Pope wrote, where the poet John Masefield lived earlier in the century, sits on a slope in this charming part of the Cotswolds almost completely enclosed by dense foliage which in summer stands in the way in every direction of possible views. Almost immediately there is a path on the right running down to the left of the church, with a cottage over the wall to the left. At the bottom there is a junction and the main path, the one you want, shears away to the left; but it is worthwhile making a short excursion along a short strip of gravel into the field ahead for a glimpse of the topiary avenue to the right, a row of vegetable chimneys. Return to the correct path, and as it widens, after passing a couple of cottages on the right, turn right down a narrow path between stone walls.

The path turns to a track as it runs between thick bushes. Leave the cottages behind and soon a meadow appears to the right, sloping down to the valley bottom and the River Frome. The path comes to an end at a stile.

Go over the stile into the field and bear left. Pass a water trough on the left, and then take a diagonal line down to the right of a tree, passing what appears to be a small redundant pumping station on the right. The path descends to bring you to a stile which is not immediately evident, although it lies someway to the right of the gateway you will see to your left.

Go over the stile. A few steps immediately afterwards descend to the top of the old Sapperton canal tunnel. All around there is debris like an abandoned Roman temple; and there is an unprotected drop into the canal on the right. Go across the top of the tunnel and bear right to descend to the main path which runs alongside the disused Thames and Severn Canal which is to the right. The tunnel was the longest in the country at the time of its completion in 1789 and was last used in 1911. So impressive was the engineering involved in its construction that the King himself came to admire it.

The path is clear. Passing a tumbledown building on the left, it continues without any danger of confusion all the way to the Daneway Inn, with the bottom of the waterless canal carpeted in plants, the far bank bright with flowering hawthorn. Just before the pub is a halter stile. Cross this and pass to the left of the inn as the path rises up to the road. Turn right along the road and then turn left to continue along the tow path with the canal now to the left.

The drawing shows the Northern end of the canal tunnel.
The tunnel is 2¼ miles long and was a very busy and important
route between Lechlade on the Thames and Framilode on the Severn.

There are meadows rising to the right but the workings of the canal to the left are very much more in evidence here, with tree roots forcing their way through the brickwork – you pass lock after lock with the old timbers still doing a job and the grooves where the lock gates slid still visible. Revealed in this woodland, green and of tropical density, it is like the discovery of a lost, enigmatic civilisation.

9

Continue on until a narrow wooden bridge with metal railings spans the canal and takes you across after which you turn right to continue now with the canal on the right. Keep going through the reek of wild garlic until you come to a red-brick hump-back bridge. Follow the path under the bridge, looking back at the plaque marking the date of construction, 1784, and the initials of, presumably, the designer. The path continues to the left of the canal. Soon views of hills appear to the right, and a couple of rusting sheds. Eventually you will pass over a halter stile. Trees tower to the right. You enter a tunnel of overhanging branches. Open meadow appears to the left and later to the right. Pass through a kissing gate and then another.

A cottage appears before you, with a small wooden dovecote attached to its flank. Pass to the right of this, with kitchen garden on the other bank of the canal, pass the high stone wall on the left and beyond it the steep forested side of the valley. Keep going and pass another cottage until the path emerges onto a wider track by means of a gate. Pass yet another cottage on the left, after which a small arched footbridge crosses the canal on the right. Ignore this and bear left around the cottage and then turn sharp left up the flank of the hill to a stile. The path curls left and then right to then level out across a sloping meadow. Behind is quite an impressive view down to the bridge and the path hugging the canal.

Cross the meadow to a stile. The path on the other side rises shortly to a railway line. Take the utmost care in crossing this, not only look to the left and right but listen intently, too. On the other side a narrow path climbs through the undergrowth to bring you to a road by a cottage. Turn right and then immediately left to follow the lane as it rises towards the church. The road eventually curls left (although there is an overgrown short cut on the left which cuts off the corner) around the Italianate, 19th century church and then levels out at a junction to bring you into Frampton Mansell. Keep straight on with a fine view across the valley to the left until you come to the 17th century Crown Inn, formerly, apparently, a slaughter house on the corner of a road which runs down to the left.

Again, carry straight on along the road, passing the pub on the left. Keep going, the road rising not too steeply, until you come to a footpath sign on the left, which you ignore. Then the road descends and corkscrews. Ignore the footpath signs on the left here too and keep going for some little while until a substantial opening appears on the left, probably marked by a couple of large logs.

Take the path until after a short time the path forks, the main path appearing to bear to the left, the right path bearing right into the woods. Go to the right along a muddy woodland path which eventually emerges into the light, mixed plantation appearing to the left, the road above you to the right (evident from the occasional drone of a passing car) until, after quite some time of gradual descent, it opens up at a clearing. Follow the track as it bears left and then right to emerge at a road.

Turn right and follow the road as it rises to the edge of Sapperton village. Turn left at a junction and follow the pavement past the school until the church reappears.

'Legging it" through a Canal Tunnel.

The SAPPERTON - FRAMPTON MANSELL Walk

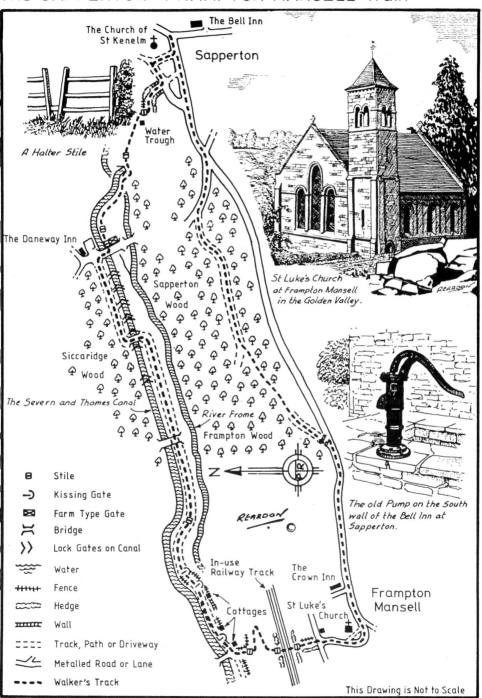

The Bell Inn

The Church of
St Kenelm

Sapperton

Water
Trough

A Halter Stile

The Daneway Inn

St Luke's Church
at Frampton Mansell
in the Golden Valley.

Sapperton
Wood

Siccaridge
Wood

The Severn and Thames Canal

River Frome

Frampton Wood

The old Pump on the South
wall of the Bell Inn at
Sapperton.

REARDON

In-use
Railway Track

The
Crown Inn

Frampton
Mansell

Cottages

St Luke's
Church

日	Stile
⇁	Kissing Gate
⊠	Farm Type Gate
⌒	Bridge
⟩⟩	Lock Gates on Canal
〜	Water
﬩	Fence
⌇	Hedge
⊞	Wall
⁝⁝⁝⁝	Track, Path or Driveway
⌐	Metalled Road or Lane
● ● ●	Walker's Track

This Drawing is Not to Scale

11

3 Bourton on the Water

Distance: 4 miles
Time: About 2 hours
Map: OS Pathfinder 1090 (SP 01/11, Northleach and Andoversford) and 1067 (SP 02/12 Stow-on-the-Wold) or OS Landranger 163 (Cheltenham and Cirencester).
Starting Point: Grid ref 169208
Terrain: A flat walk. Some patches of mud hinder progress but only briefly.
Refreshments: Wide variety available in Bourton.

Here is an opportunity to visit a Cotswold village (more of a town in reality): Bourton-on-the-Water, which is singularly unappealing during the summer when overrun by trippers but rather an attractive place when visible. This walk takes you on a circuit of the chain of lakes that lie just outside the village.

Bourton-on-the-Water is the so-called 'Venice of the Cotswolds' on account of the River Windrush which runs rather sedately beneath a quintet of bridges that do, in their simple, graceful way, bear a fleeting resemblance to the Rialto bridge in that Italian city.

It presents a charming scene when there are few people around. Furthermore, there are several items of interest which are of course aimed at entertaining the hordes that come here in the summer, but which are worth spending time over if you are so inclined – the Cotswold Motor Museum, the Model Railway, the Model Village and Birdland.

The starting point for the walk is the main car park on Station Road (although you may find a parking place along the main street on a good day; in which case make your way to the car park via the walled path running alongside the Dial House Hotel).

From the car park go to the road, keeping to the right of the garage, and cross over to the path on the other side. Turn right until, almost immediately, you will come to a footpath on the left.

Go along here, to the right of a bus depot, and to the left of a meadow, until at its end, you come to the curve of a narrow lane, opposite a cemetery.

Turn right and follow the lane (a no-through road but which just might bear traffic), with views to the right to the houses of Bourton and the hills beyond – already the bustle of Bourton seems some distance away. Ignore the footpath that bears away to the right and stick to the road to pass a large expanse of allotments on the left and then a wall, which, uncharacteristically, uses mortar, to the right, beyond which is an attractive ornamental garden. The lane declines to a gravel track after a while. Gaps in the hedge to the left afford glimpses of a ridge; pass a gate to the left and a cottage to the right and keep going as a house appears on the lower horizon directly in front of you.

This marks a split in the path. Take the left fork as it curves left between hedgerows with the ridge before you. Small lakes make their first appearance to the left and soon you come to a gate, in fact two gates, but go through the gap to the right of the gate in front of you as a lake, surrounded by willows, appears now on the right. Beyond, continue for not more than about fifty yards until a path appears on your right, just before a gate marked 'private'.

Take this narrow path which runs between two hedges either side of which are lakes, steely blue in the light, fringed by wind-brushed rushes and grasses. Follow the path as it curves to the left, amid brambles, the lake still to the left, hedge to the right, and crosses a small stream of clear water, the bottom covered in a web of pondweed. Ignore a small bridge on the right (leading to barbed wire) and instead follow the path as it turns smartly right to a gate and another bridge to a meadow.

Go over this into a wide open meadow and head more or less straight across, though heading slightly to the right to a stile and gate inserted into a hedge. Once across this you will be in another meadow. Trees, marking the course of the mighty Dikler are ahead. Bear right to where the river sharply curves away and then follow this picturesque and fast-flowing stream to a bridge; cross this to quickly arrive at another, right by the old mill. Beyond this is a greensward between, on the right, a row of trees and a tennis court, and on the left a high wall with rather fortified lines of zig-zags and bulwarks, seemingly ready to repel invaders and withstand a siege.

At its end you will come to a kissing gate. Go through to a rippling meadow, with its smartly-trimmed hedge afore you. Then cross a stile (pausing in mid air to catch a glimpse of the old mill) and bear right along a stony drive. With hedge on your right and a fence to the left, follow this as it heads in the direction of a gentle slope and then curves, eventually, to the right. Up on the ridge you will see a few farm buildings and Little Rissington's solitary church; ignore a sign on the left indicating a footpath across a magnificently-furrowed field, and eventually set foot on the corner of a metalled lane which, to the right, leads to a sewerage plant. Not surprisingly, this item is not on the route. Continue straight ahead until you fetch up at a junction with the road to Bourton, noting that the church continues to peep over the brow of the hill on the left.

Turn right at the road (there is a pavement), opposite Home Farm, and continue until a road appears on the left, just as the pavement comes to an end in front of a handsome house. Cross over to follow this narrow lane, posted for Great Rissington, for quite some way. Hemmed in by hedge and trees (interestingly there are almost no stone walls around here) it will take you past a sloping meadow on the left and a gate on the right, soon after which the road will curve around to the right. Ignore a footpath sign and a little bridge on the right; and then another footpath sign as the road curves left and right. Then it straightens up to eventually pass an entrance to a field on the right with a barn in it. Soon after, on the right, opposite a field that slopes up to woodland, is a stile (indicated by a sign on the left hand side of the road). This takes you into a field.

Continue in a straight line, with a tall hedge to your right, through a gateway into a second field. The river will appear at your side on the right and then a wooden bridge across it. Cross this and turn immediately to the left with the river on your left and meadows to the right. Follow the narrow path as it curves to the right, leaving the river, and then to the left to bring you to a gate.

Go through this to a meadow into which is inserted a small, pristine, lake. There is sure to be a sprinkling of birds here, perhaps even flocks of them. The activity is a marvel for, as well as the usual coots and moorhens, you may see Great Crested

Grebes on patrol; swans (black and white) searching for food, their heads under water and their posteriors rising up like ice floes; and little stormy whorls of petrels (or something of the sort), their underwings glinting as they spiral. Keep the lake to your right and follow its contours around to the right until you come to a gate and stile. Go through this and continue walking to the left of the lake, as the River Windrush appears to the left.

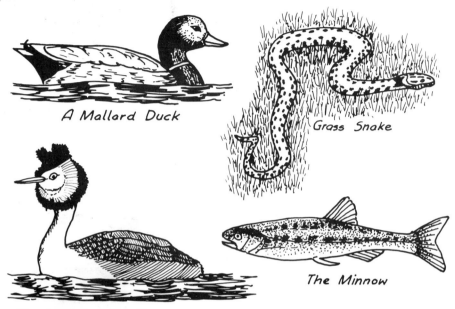

A Mallard Duck

Grass Snake

The Minnow

The Great Crested Grebe

Not long after meeting the second and larger lake you should make a diversion to keep to the right of way – take a path on the left across the river to then turn immediately right. This will take you behind the green boathouse after which you may turn right to recross the river and bring you once again to the edge of the lake (an object more easily achieved by remaining on the lake side of the river and walking in front of the boathouse, though there are signs to tell you that is not appreciated).

Once you have reached the end of the lake, keep it to your right and then bear left to cross an all but disappeared cattle grid onto a track. Follow this between meadows towards houses and pass through a gate. Before you is the main road. Cross this, turn right and very soon turn left over a stile into a field, houses to the left. Traverse this to another stile in the corner as a lake appears away to the right beyond some trees. Vault over the stile, cross a small bridge to the lakeside, and then continue for a few yards to another stile. The path on the other side will lead between lakes, with, on the right, what look like old stone stables.

Another lake appears to the right, followed by a series of smaller lakes or ponds; modern houses appear on the left, behind a stone wall. Before long the path comes to an end at a stile by a gate. On the other side is a lane that you will recognise – carry straight on here to the cemetery and bear left at the corner to bring you back to the car park.

The BOURTON on the WATER Walk

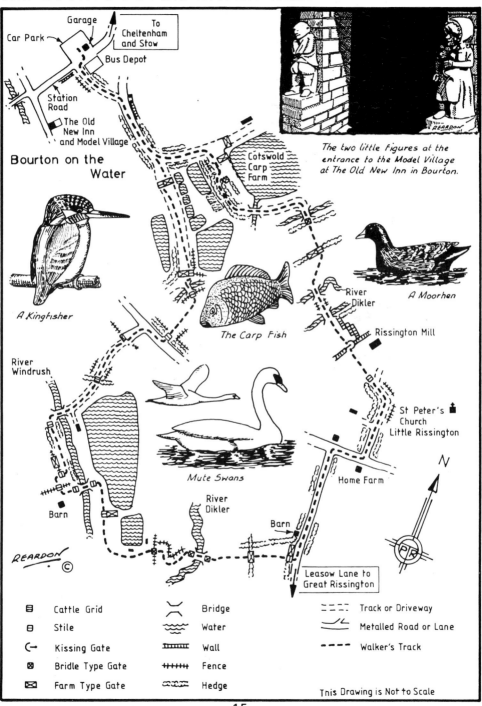

Garage

Car Park

To Cheltenham and Stow

Bus Depot

Station Road

The Old New Inn and Model Village

Bourton on the Water

Cotswold Carp Farm

The two little figures at the entrance to the Model Village at The Old New Inn in Bourton.

A Kingfisher

River Windrush

The Carp Fish

River Dikler

A Moorhen

Rissington Mill

St Peter's Church
Little Rissington

Mute Swans

River Dikler

Barn

Home Farm

Barn

Leasow Lane to Great Rissington

REARDON ©

	Cattle Grid	⌣	Bridge	⌐ ⌐ ⌐	Track or Driveway
	Stile	〜	Water		Metalled Road or Lane
↳	Kissing Gate	▥	Wall	- - -	Walker's Track
⊗	Bridle Type Gate	+++++	Fence		
⊠	Farm Type Gate	ᗧᗧᗧ	Hedge	This Drawing is Not to Scale

N

15

4 Bredon's Norton

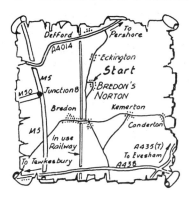

Distance: 4¹/4 miles
Time: 2 hours of continuous walking
Map: OS Pathfinder SO 83/93 (Tewkesbury) and SO 84/94 (Pershore)
Starting Point: Grid ref 931381
Terrain: A little road but mostly farm track and woodland and hillside paths. There will be some mud but the going is pretty firm on the whole.
Refreshments: The Royal Oak in Bredon is nearest.

Bredon Hill is a notable landmark in the area, offering what are surely some of the finest views in all England.

The climb to its summit, therefore, is worthwhile – particularly as the balance of the walk is simple and undemanding and the route clearly defined.

A clear day will provide an admirable backdrop but choose a day when the matinal mist gives way to clear blue skies and views to the farthest horizon – 'Bredon Hill doth clear appear, ye men of the Vale have naught to fear'. There is one slight drawback in all this: the absence of any place of refreshment en route. There is, however, a pub about two miles away in Bredon.

Bredon's Norton is a quiet and pretty village with a remarkable variety of houses and farm buildings. The church, with its twin clocks, dates back to the 12th century, although the nave had to be rebuilt in 1886 in the wake of a fire.

Park with care where you are able and seek out the village hall with its humble bell tower on a corner at the junction of the two roads. From the hall, walk up the lane towards Bredon Hill, with the church to your left, passing the Westmancote footpath on your right.

At the top of the lane you will pass a couple of modern houses in sallow brick and come into a junction. Turn right in the direction of Bredon Hill as indicated.

Pass the sign that forbids parking and enter what amounts to a drive, which passes a 14th century thatched tithe barn on the left, said to have been used by Shakespeare for the staging of some of his plays and then the imposing 16th century manor with its lonely- looking arch, inscribed 1585, upholding a pair of handsome wrought iron gates.

The drive passes these buildings and curves round to the left, passes a gate into a meadow on the right, and brings you to a farm gate with a little metal gate to its left, beyond which are some farm buildings in black. A track runs away to the right. Ignore this and enter the field, pass to the right of the buildings and head up the field, with its corrugations and grazing sheep. The hill rises about you.

As you mount the hill, walking towards some woodland, you will see a gateway just to the right of a telegraph pole. Head for this, noticing as you do so a low and perhaps ancient stone wall on your left that appears to enclose nothing more than a large amount of dense undergrowth.

Go through the gate, ensuring that the sheep, which have a tendency to cluster around you wearing looks of blank expectation, do not exit with you.

Ahead of you the trail is quite clear and essentially you are to continue walking up the gradient of the field. On your left some cottages will appear; and then the mass of Norton Park. In front of you a clump of some seven trees will appear. Keep to the right and head towards another gate, which may well be open.

Pass through the gate and continue up what is by now becoming most definitely a hill, something that is not only clear from the effort required to walk but also from the views that are appearing behind.

A gate will appear on the right leading into a sort of paddock. Ignore this and head for another gate that stands a little way up beyond it. Pass through it by means of the stubby stile at its side and find yourself in an area of coarse and rugged hillside, bestrewn with a variety of bushes, shrubs and trees and lumps and outcrops.

The path, however, is clearly defined and takes you ever skywards, passing the track on the right which is to be disregarded.

The path is undeniably a little on the steep side for a short while but sublime views are beginning to open up around you as the path rises above the level of the woodland.

This is the true splendour of Bredon Hill. Its singularity and that of the surrounding villages has poetic resonances. Thus, one of John Masefield's most famous lines is: *All the land from Ludlow Town, To Bredon Church's spire.* Inevitably, Bredon figures in A E Housman's A Shropshire Lad, in the 21st poem In Summertime on Bredon.

So the hill's natural beauty is enhanced by association with poetic vision. It is not surprising, for it covers a vast area and commands attention from above and below.

The trail continues clearly and curves to the right, aslant the breast of the hill, fetching you up at another gate. Go through (a sign informs you that you have just left an area designated by the Nature Conservancy Council as of special scientific interest and indeed you may catch sight of deer or buzzards or woodpeckers) into another area of dense, thorny bush and follow the obvious trail as it continues to bear right and rise towards a distant ridge, although the slope is much less severe at this juncture.

You will seem to be heading in the general direction of some fir trees and fairly soon

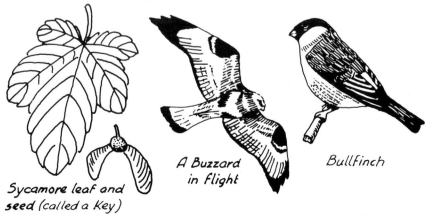

Sycamore leaf and seed (called a Key)

A Buzzard in flight

Bullfinch

the path will present you with a gateway and a sign that informs you in no uncertain terms that you are not to transgress.

Turn left here and follow a track as it passes a number of fir trees on the right and brings you into a corner of a large field, the flatness of which tells you that you are pretty much at the summit of the hill. Turn immediately right and follow the right hand margin of the field until you arrive at an apex almost opposite to the point where you entered the field. At this juncture you will notice to the right a barn amid acres of field. Go through the gate in the corner onto an obvious track that will take you immediately past a small crater, or the remains of a quarry, on your left. To your right is a stone wall behind which is woodland.

Continue until, in the far right hand corner, you come to a bridle gate on the right that will lead you onto the edge of the escarpment where a path threads its way through a strip of woodland, the Warren, with an open field to the right.

There are two paths here, one amid the trees, another at the edge of the field – the former is likely to be less muddy. Keep going until the path steers around a sunken gully that will appear below you to the left and which leads towards a gate. To continue the walk, you should take this but if you wish to visit a local landmark, the Bambury Tower, which is a short distance from here, then you should continue on the path through the trees and then return to the gully. Enter the gully and vault over the gate that is fixed between stone walls. The path leads downwards and soon the gully sides give way to Bredon's lower, more open slopes. The track peters out but the path remains obvious as it winds between the earthen dunes towards a metal gate.

You have a choice of gates but take the middle one, just by a stone pillar and enter a large field.

As you descend in the general direction of the woodland in front of you, a curious set of funnels appear to the right and overlooking all, Mr Parson's folly, a bump on the razor sharp skyline behind you.

Head over the main hump of the field and down towards a gateway in the bottom right hand corner next to an arched tree stump. Go over the stile to the right of the gate to find yourself on a substantial parkland track. Turn left and walk down the track. Pass through a gate and then bear left across the meadow, keeping to the right of the brook and noticing the obscure stone slab bridge as you do so.

Woollas Hall will have loomed up out of the hollow by now, surrounded by a forest of ornamental trees and shrubs. As you head for the hall, a stile will appear and let you onto the driveway, where you turn left, walk across a cattle grid and enter the grounds. Thread your way through this little domain, following the route as it takes you through the grounds. As you leave the hall behind, the path is now almost unmistakable all the way to Bredon's Norton.

Ignore the branch on the left that leads to the lodge. The path curves past St Catherine's Farm, with an old barn on the left, and emerges through a gate to bear left around the girth of the hill. All the time you are making a gradual descent, preparing for a final approach to Bredon's Norton.

Then the path rises briefly and a barn appears among the trees to the right. The track leaves the estate and becomes a tarmac lane which you follow as it descends.

You will pass the entrance to a field on the left and then an enclosed patch of woodland. The lane curves around it to the left and soon the houses of Bredon's Norton appear.

Keep going until you come to a junction, with the entrance to Norton Park on the left. Turn right and descend past some charming cottages to the heart of the village.

The BREDON'S NORTON Walk

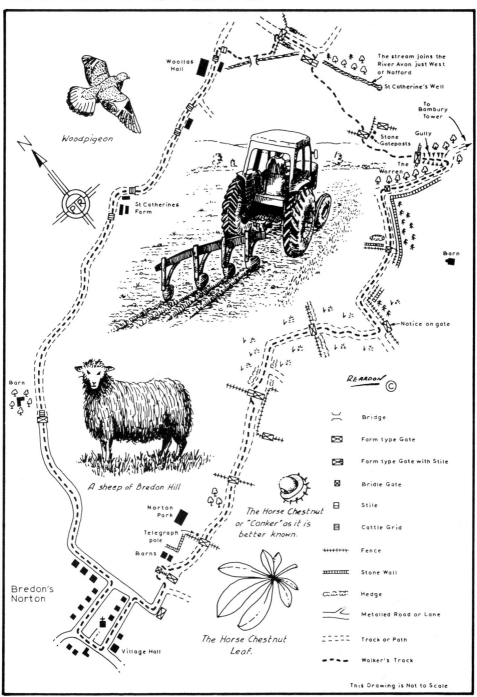

The stream joins the River Avon just West of Nafford

St Catherine's Well

To Bambury Tower

Woollas Hall

Woodpigeon

Stone Gateposts

Gully

The Warren

St Catherines Farm

Barn

Notice on gate

Barn

REARDON ©

A sheep of Bredon Hill

Norton Park

Telegraph pole

Barns

The Horse Chestnut or "Conker" as it is better known.

Bredon's Norton

Village Hall

The Horse Chestnut Leaf.

‿	Bridge
⊠	Farm type Gate
⊠	Farm type Gate with Stile
⊠	Bridle Gate
日	Stile
日	Cattle Grid
+++++++	Fence
▭▭▭▭	Stone Wall
ഝഝ	Hedge
～	Metalled Road or Lane
- - - -	Track or Path
•-•-•-	Walker's Track

This Drawing is Not to Scale

19

5 Wainlode Hill

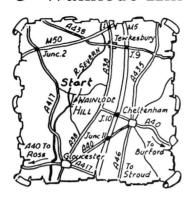

Distance: 4½ miles
Time: 2 hours of continuous walking
Map: OS Pathfinder SO 82/92 (Cheltenham)
Starting Point: Grid ref 849259
Terrain: On the whole the going is likely to be soft, since it is mostly grassland and earthen paths. There are some gradients at the start.
Refreshments: The Red Lion pub at Wainlode is a delightful hostelry at the base of the hill on the riverbank.

In many ways, this is a surprising walk. Although the river is never far away, much of the time you will be walking through woodland or across high fields, from where there are marvellous views to be enjoyed of the surrounding countryside. There is, however, plenty of opportunity to enjoy life on and along Britain's longest river. It is a walk that allows complete relaxation as, although there is a pub en route, there is otherwise very little sign of habitation.

You should park with care in the vicinity of the delightful red brick Red Lion pub at Wainlode, at the base of the hill on the banks of the Severn. Cross the road from the pub and bear left over a stile, by a sign indicating the Severn Way, into a sloping field in which there are a few fruit trees.

As you make your way up the slope, fine views already begin to open up of the silvery sweep of the river, with its swans, of the plain beyond the pub and of the surrounding hills. Head towards another stile that you can see in front of you at the top of the field to the right, taking care to keep an eye on the crumbling cliff edge.

This stile takes you into another field, with a grass strip of a path along its right-hand margin, in the shadow of a number of flowering bushes. Follow this as it continues to rise slightly up to another stile in the corner. This will take you into another grassy field by woodland. Follow the right edge of the field as it rises more steeply, ignoring any invitation to enter the woodland that lies between you and the river. Then you will come to another stile in the corner.

Cross this into yet another field, ignoring a gateway into a smaller field on the right. Continue up and forward between an isolated tree on the left and hedgerow on the right. It is worth looking behind you from time to time to see the views that continue to open up far and wide. Keep going in the same direction along the edge of the field littered with horse jumps, until woodland on both sides begins to close in. Soon the grass will give way to a dirt track which will take you over a crossroads of tracks and then to a point where the two areas of woodland come together at the apex of the tapering field. Pass through a gate onto an obvious track, with a barn to the right, which stretches away across a field before you.

Trees continue to accompany you on the left but then they fall away and leave you with divine views across the Vale of Gloucester to the city of Gloucester, Cheltenham

20

and the Cotswolds. The track runs clear and true across the field until it meets a couple of trees, one of which shades a triangular point. At this juncture, the river appears below you to the right and the views round about border on the spectacular. The track bears a little to the right, with hedge on the left and open fields to the right and begins to descend Sandhurst Hill in the direction of the river.

As the track descends and becomes flecked with red brick and the tower of Gloucester Cathedral seems ever closer to the left, the buildings of Brawn Farm will appear before you. The track takes you past some large modern constructions on the right, then becomes a causeway running between a couple of ponds haunted by duck and moorhen, before debouching onto a metalled road by an attractive white house. Sandhurst is to the left but turn right here, passing a ruined red-brick barn on the right.

Soon, the lane gives way to uneven track and begins to weave its way down between hedgerow towards the river and the spire of the church of Ashleworth.

The road becomes deeper and the hedges higher and higher and then it bottoms out, so that the presence of the river seems imminent. But this is a deception, because the lane rises again and wanders on through the spongy meadows of the flood plain. The air is filled with the pungent smells of the countryside. Then you will come to a pond on the left. Just after, on the right, is a stile, over which you will be bounding on your way back to Wainlode. Ahead of you, however, is a short rise and then the river.

A Princess 32 Motor Cruiser on the River Severn

On the other side of the river is the Boat Inn and, beyond it, the delightful village of Ashleworth, one of the finest groups of medieval buildings on the Severn. The church is of ancient origins and nearby is a house that dates back to 1460 and a tithe barn, also of the 15th century, that is some 125 feet in length. The Boat Inn marks the location of the quay that has served the ferry between Ashleworth and Sandhurst for centuries.

The Jelf family have owned the ferry rights since 1643 when King Charles I, fleeing the siege of Gloucester, was rowed across the river at this spot by a Mr Jelf. The grateful king bestowed upon him and his descendants the privilege of enjoying the ferry monopoly in perpetuity. Jelfs continue to run the Boat Inn but you are likely to experience some difficulty in getting across the river these days and may have to watch longingly from the opposite bank.

So, return to the stile on the other side of the hump and go over it into the field that runs along the banks of the Severn. The path, the Severn Way, is quite distinct, being a sort of spinal column that runs slightly off the riverbank. The Severn Way, opened in 1989 as part of the centenary celebrations of Gloucestershire County Council, runs between Tewkesbury and Shepperdine. As you walk back towards the hill, you will see the track that brought you down to Brawn Farm above you to the right. This first is a long curving field but will bring you eventually to a stile which will take you into another smaller field. This in turn will take you into another field and then another. On your right, on the side of the hill, is a large group of similar trees with wispy tops like dandelions.

Eventually the route will take you over another stile onto a woodland path. Just before that, you may come across some electrified fence which you must negotiate with care. The path is level at first and the trees on either side of it filled with birdsong. To your left, the river laps gently at the roots of the trees.

After a while, the path will rise slightly and then level out again before coming to a substantial flight of steps that climb straight up to the edge of a field by a fence. Turn left here and follow the path, which will then enter more woodland and eventually bring you to a stile. Over the stile and you are on the edge of a field where you trod earlier. Turn left here and use the succession of stiles to take you down the hill and back to where you started.

The Red Lion Inn at Wainlode Hill.

22

The WAINLODE HILL Walk

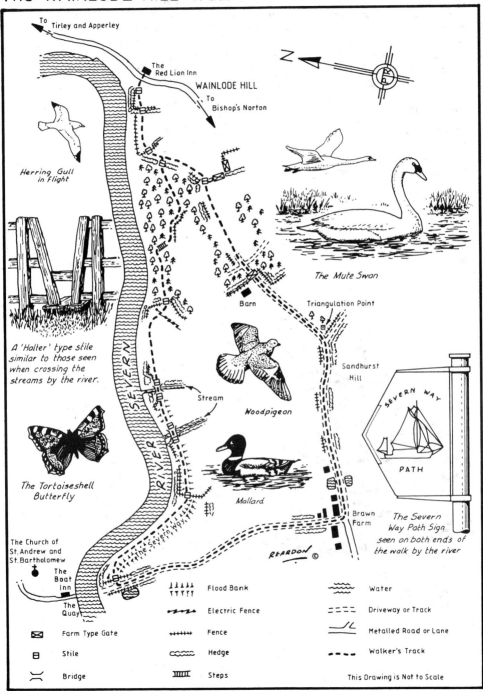

To Tirley and Apperley

The Red Lion Inn

WAINLODE HILL

To Bishop's Norton

Herring Gull in Flight

A 'Halter' type stile similar to those seen when crossing the streams by the river.

The Tortoiseshell Butterfly

The Church of St. Andrew and St. Bartholomew

The Boat Inn

The Quay

RIVER SEVERN

Stream

Woodpigeon

Mallard

The Mute Swan

Barn

Triangulation Point

Sandhurst Hill

The Severn Way

Brawn Farm

SEVERN WAY PATH

The Severn Way Path Sign seen on both ends of the walk by the river

REARDON ©

⊠	Farm Type Gate	
⊟	Stile	
⟩⟨	Bridge	

Flood Bank	
Electric Fence	
Fence	
Hedge	
Steps	

Water	
Driveway or Track	
Metalled Road or Lane	
Walker's Track	

This Drawing is Not to Scale

23

6 Bulls Cross-Slad

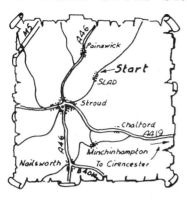

Distance: 4¹/₂ miles
Time: 2¹/₂ hours of continuous walking
Map: OS Pathfinder 1113 (SO 80/90, Stroud)
Starting Point: Grid ref 878089
Terrain: A lot of field walking, some of which is fairly steep, though of short duration. A little woodland and some road and track.
Refreshments: The Woolpack at Slad.

Here we tackle another the area around Slad which for one particular reason – associations with the modern classic, Cider with Rosie, by Laurie Lee – has come to be considered the essence of the Cotswolds.

There is adequate parking space in the lay-by at Bulls Cross, a meeting point of ancient tracks, on the left hand side of the road as you travel in the direction of Stroud. From here walk forward a fraction (still in the direction of Stroud) until you see a lane on the left, disappearing fairly steeply through a gateway down towards a meadow, passing a hedge on the left.

As you descend, views open up along the twisting valley to the right, covered here and there with patches of dense woodland, sprinklings of cattle and sheep, and the occasional farmhouse. Continue through another gateway, as a greenhouse appears just to the right and then the outlines of farm buildings. The lane curves down to the right to enter the yard but just before you reach the first building turn left to go over a stile into a steep meadow.

Follow this down, where it is quite worn, to the bottom right-hand corner where you will see a gate, with Slad Brook running close by. Continue ahead into the next field and proceed ever up, rather steeply, with the hedge to your right. The roof of a stone cottage will appear to the right and then a gate will appear in front of you. Pass through this onto a track, where a sign post indicates Bulls Cross. Turn left here.

Continue to ascend, though more gently now, with undergrowth and hedge on your right and the meadow and valley to the left. Fairly soon you will come to a junction of tracks, where you bear right and then continue towards another junction as houses appear below you to the right.

At the junction turn right again to walk along a country lane. Pass a farm on the left, the road descending quite sharply, with a fine view directly in front of you of the sinuous S-shaped valley. The track bottoms out by the old mill, with its ungainly shape. Follow the road, with steep-sided meadows on the right and the stream to the left. The village of Slad will then become evident ahead of you to the right. This small, unremarkable-seeming village is distinguished for its associations with Laurie Lee, who was born in 1914.

His first book, Cider with Rosie, is the story of a Cotswold childhood, told in a lyrical style that is inventive and evocative, far more than a simple memoir. The Cotswolds happen to be the scene for the book, but it is really a book about growing up. His other books furthermore, most famously 'As I Walked Out One Midsummer Morning', are every bit as entertaining and although he is celebrated as an author and poet, many consider that his skills are underrated.

If you want to visit Slad, where refreshment may be obtained at the Woolpack Inn, you should remain on the road and then return to the pond to continue the walk. The stream on the left will soon run into a large pond (or a small lake, depending on your point of view), its slightly murky waters covered in flotillas of leaves and raiding parties of coots and moorhens. Just after this, on the left, just before some buildings, take the footpath which runs beside railings to a gate. A stile alongside the gate will take you into the next field. Go up its side, with hedge and a gateway on the right, until, in the top right-hand corner, a stile will take you onto a woodland path with meadow to the right and a steep bank on the left.

The path will flatten out as it curves left to a stile. Go over this into a field and go ahead bearing slightly to the left, keeping to the line of the hedge. Then a stile will appear before you. Go over this, with views of Slad to the right and Stroud ahead in the distance and continue ahead once again along the top of a sloping meadow. Pass a gate on the left in the direction of another gate, beyond which is a cottage. As you approach the gate in front of you, pass to the left of a small orchard; pass through the gate and then, almost immediately, another. This will take you onto a track which passes through cottages and farmhouses and then curves around to the left by a stone wall on the right. The track then begins to rise but you should take the path that leads down to the right through the trees.

This will bring you to a stile on the right. Over this into a field and head straight across to another stile in the middle, overlooked by the farmhouse at the top of the field to the right. Over this one, too, to head a little left to a halter stile and bridge in the corner. After crossing this into a field, turn right and then bear left over the brow of the hill to head for a gate on the left at the top of the field. Go through, cross a track and go over a stile into another sloping meadow.

Ahead of you is a fringe of yew bushes, partially concealing a cottage. Head just to the left of the bushes where you will find a stile. Cross this onto a track and turn left.

Continue to a crossroads and bear right along a road that descends and curves down to the right. It descends past the stream and then rises up, passing a footpath sign on the right, to the main road.

At the main road turn left and follow the road, making use of the thoughtfully-provided pavement, for quite some way. Away to the left are pleasant views of the steep-sided valley slopes. Pass a gateway and a field with a couple of sheds in it, littered with abandoned machinery, visible beyond the hedgerow and trees. Then Hazel Mill will appear none too obviously, below to the left, just as you pass the sign for Stroud, the town itself clearly visible strung out along the sides of the valley. Just opposite, on the other side of the road, are a few muddy steps leading up to a stile. Cross this into a steep field.

Head straight up, keeping to the right-hand side until you come to another stile. Go over this and turn left to go across the angle of the slope among the bushes and brambles. This will open up into another field where you turn immediately right to head up towards a large spinney. Keeping to the left of the trees will fetch you up by a gate below a farmhouse. Go through this into another field to follow a path in the direction of the house. Before long go left over what passes for a stile into yet another steep field and head diagonally up to the top right-hand corner where you will find a gate.

Go through the gate onto a concrete track, which you cross; and then, keeping a barn to the left, bear right on a track which will take you behind the farmhouse. Keep on this track with the house now beneath you to the right until, just before the track curves left to rise up towards the trees, a huge ladder stile will take you over the fence into the neighbouring field on the left.

Go up the field to another similar stile and go over this onto a metalled road – Folly Lane. Turn right and keep to the lane. Pass an organic conservation area, Folly Acres, on the right after a short while and continue to ignore all footpaths to left or right. The lane becomes more of a track as it passes near cottages and through a farmyard. Eventually you will come to a junction, with paths or tracks going away to the left and right. Treat these with disdain and instead push on over a stile into a field. Keep to its left hand margin until you come to a gate at the corner of a dense thatch of woodland. Go through onto an obvious path, veined with roots, which leads you unerringly

A ladder stile near Wickridge Farm.

through the trees. Although the path opens up from time to time to a glade, and although there are other paths coming and going, left and right, by continuing in the same direction you cannot go wrong.

Eventually, across the valley to the left, you will be able to see majestic Painswick, and its sublime church spire; and then you will pass a stone pillar and a broken gate before emerging once again at Bulls Cross.

The BULLS CROSS – SLAD Walk

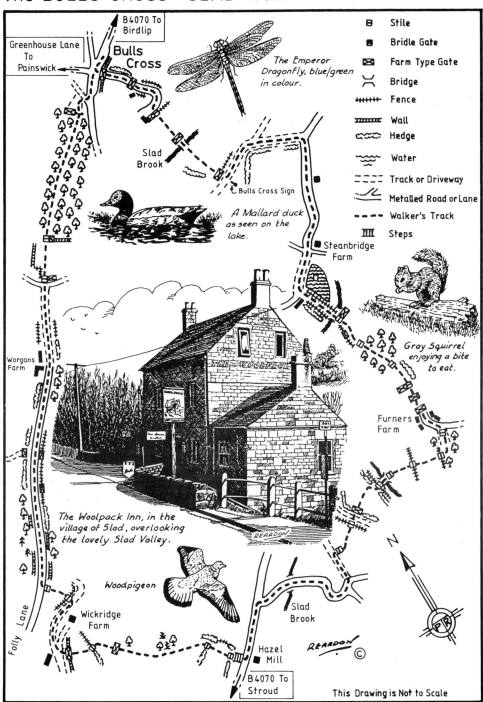

B4070 To Birdlip

Greenhouse Lane To Painswick

Bulls Cross

The Emperor Dragonfly, blue/green in colour.

Stile ⊟
Bridle Gate ▣
Farm Type Gate ⊠
Bridge ⋈
Fence ┼┼┼┼┼
Wall ▭
Hedge ∽
Water ≈
Track or Driveway ‑ ‑ ‑ ‑
Metalled Road or Lane ⌇
Walker's Track ▪ ▪ ▪
Steps ⫼

Slad Brook

Bulls Cross Sign

A Mallard duck as seen on the lake.

Steanbridge Farm

Gray Squirrel enjoying a bite to eat.

Worgans Farm

THE WOOLPACK

Furners Farm

The Woolpack Inn, in the village of Slad, overlooking the lovely Slad Valley.

REARDON

N

Woodpigeon

Slad Brook

Folly Lane

Wickridge Farm

Hazel Mill

REARDON ©

B4070 To Stroud

This Drawing is Not to Scale

27

7 Bisley-Bournes Green

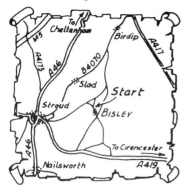

Distance: 4³/4 miles
Time: 2 hrs 25 mins
Map: OS Pathfinder 1113 (SO 80/90, Stroud)
Starting Point: Grid ref 903061
Terrain: Fields for the most part, with a little woodland, some farm track and a fair number of quiet lanes.
Refreshments: The Bear Inn at Bisley and the Butcher's Arms at Oakridge. There is also an excellent tea shop at Bisley.

WE find ourselves in the deep south of the Cotswolds with good reason, for, on the whole, this area does not attract the crowds which buzz around the honeypots of the north. And yet, whilst it is true that the picturesque quality which bounds to the north and northeast is less in evidence here, these southern reaches have quite a separate charm of their own.

The walk begins in the village of Bisley and it is suggested that you park along the road which is at right angles to the main street, opposite the post office, which leads up to the Bear Inn, an early 19th-century lock up with two doors and the appearance of a small chapel.

Bisley is a village of considerable interest. Historically it developed upon the wealth of the wool clothiers who built some magnificent houses like Over Court, with its 18th-century gazebo, and Jaynes Court just to the southwest of the church. The church is notable for its spire and its 13th-century 'Poor Soul's Light', the only outdoor example in the country.

Apart from Bisley's intrinsic winsomness, there are a couple of other features deserving of note. First, a curious legend suggests that Elizabeth I is buried in the churchyard. It is said that as a young girl, staying at Over Court, the young princess took ill and died. It was decided to keep her death a secret and to find a replacement; but the only red-head in the neighbourhood turned out to be a boy. It is surmised that it was he who became 'Queen Elizabeth', that being the explanation for her manly ways.

Bisley also boasts a six-sided memorial with seats which conceal an old bone hole where bones from desecrated graves were thrown. A local priest is supposed to have fallen in and died some six centuries past provoking the Pope to ban burials in Bisley for two years. Villagers had thus to trek to Bibury with their dead where there is still a plot in the churchyard called the 'Bisley Piece'.

Walk towards the post office and turn right along the main street. Pass a succession of fascinating buildings, including L'Aperitif restaurant and a tea house on the left, and the Methodist Church on the right and others whose names – the Court House, or the Old Post Office – give clues to Bisley's past life. After passing a couple of turnings down to the right, you come to a narrow road on the left leading steeply between houses up to the main road. Cross this with care and continue along a lane with fields to the right and a barn and then a nursery on the left.

Soon the road curves away to the right. Follow it around, ignoring the lane which leads straight on at the corner, and continue past a footpath on the left until you come to some cottages and farm buildings on the left. Just at the point where the farmyard comes to an end you will see, opposite a rusty gate, a footpath sign on the right, pointing into a clump of trees. In fact the path that you want leads through a rather manufactured-looking bridle gate into the field immediately preceding the trees.

Follow the left margin of the field, with splendid views across to the church on the right, until you come to another gate which will take you into another field. This time follow its right hand margin down to the bottom where you will emerge at a lane to the left of a small cottage and horse chestnut tree, with the main road beyond a junction on the right.

Cross the lane to a stile which will bring you into another meadow by some small farm buildings. Bear diagonally left up and across the meadow to a stile near the corner, just to the right of a tree. This will bring you into another field. Once again cross the field on the diagonal, heading roughly in the direction of the telegraph pole which sits in the approximate centre.

Beyond it is another stile. In the field on the other side bear straight across, taking a slight right-bearing line, which will bring you to another stile. Here, up on the southern wolds, the countryside is flatter and dourer than its sweeter northern counterpart, all human habitation hidden in cleft-like valleys.

At the timber-framed stone stile at the other side cross and then bear right across a field surrounded by high hedges. On the far side is a break in the hedge, marked with a pole surmounted by a yellow arrow, which will direct you into the next field in which you are to turn right and then bear left, following its right-hand fringe. Just before the corner you will see another stile on the right.

This will take you into a scrappy-looking meadow. Head straight across, as farm buildings appear on the right, to another stile. Go into another meadow which slopes gently down past a row of trees to another stile on the edge of woodland.

A path leads clearly and steeply down among the trees and then curves around to the right to fetch you up at the edge of another, smaller, meadow, beyond which are the clustered houses of Bournes Green. Cross this meadow, bearing slightly right, to a stile against a wall on the other side of a track. This will take you into a defile which leads away to the right between a wall on its left and a fence on its right. The path descends, crosses another stile, bears left past cottages and brings you to a clearing with a water trough to your right. Go ahead to a narrow lane and turn right and continue to a junction, where you turn left.

Continue down to another junction beyond which a bench looks out tranquilly across the narrow valley. Several roads meet here but you should take the lane which dips steeply down to the left, marked by a sign which indicates that it is unsuitable for heavy vehicles. Follow this as it descends severely, bending right and left, passing a fine house with ornamental pond on the right and a stream on the left.

The road bottoms out and then rises almost as steeply, levels out slightly, passes Lilleyhorn Farm and then rises again with a nice view along the valley to the right. Ignore the bridleway on the right as the road curves around to the left before levelling out at a junction. Cross the road and then continue along a rigidly straight road (it is tempting to see this as a Roman road since there was a Roman villa in the area but it may have been constructed during the 18th century at the time of the Inclosure Acts), passing a field with rotting chicken coops on the right, until you come to another junction. You will be turning left here but if you feel the need for refreshment there is a pub, the Butcher's Arms, a short distance along the road on the right.

If you are giving the pub a miss turn left in the direction of Waterlane, between fields of hay and corn. A farmhouse with a roof so very steeply pitched that it seems almost to be embedded in the earth will appear to the right; in front of it is a small meadow filled, perhaps, with both cows and sheep which might be taking shelter in a byre or pen made out of a pile of bales. Then you will pass a large modern house which is part of Spinneywell Nurseries.

Soon after you will come to a cluster of roads but ignore turnings on the right and continue straight ahead to a junction. Cross this and take the leftermost of two lanes marked as 'no through roads'. The lane continues straight on, passing cottages, and then a fine wall which heralds an imposing pair of gates. The road will dip down to a point where you should bear left around a farm building, ignoring the turning into Brookwoods.

You are now on a farm track which rises steadily between hedges before descending by a series of fir trees to a spinney. At the corner, where the track bears right, continue straight ahead left of the trees and at a gate turn right. Almost immediately, on the left, is a stile, leading into the field. Go over and ascend the slope to its crown and then head straight across the field in the direction of woodland. At its edge, almost invisible, is a stile.

Cross this and follow the path as it heads down through the trees to emerge into a sloping meadow. Bear left through some ferns and then quickly straighten up to descend the slope. At the bottom, among the trees, is a footbridge; but ignoring this, turn left instead and walk towards a stile.

This will take you into a thistle-strewn field. Head in the general direction of the bottom right hand corner where, hidden behind bushes, is another stile. Above you to the right is Battlescombe Farm.

Now you are in a field of long grass with a pond on the right. Keep to the same line until a point where there is a break in the trees on a fenced ridge away to the right. Turn right here and rise up to this gap which will bring you to a stile and a metalled track. Turn left here and keep on the track until you meet a road at a corner (where you walked earlier) and at which point you turn right onto a footpath which will take you to a kissing gate and a meadow on the outskirts of Bisley.

Take a diagonal line across the meadow to another gate. Go through and turn left and take the alley on the left between stone-walled small gardens until you come to railings. Dodge through these to a narrow road which needs to be crossed with care. Bear left and then immediately right to go through more railings to some steps which descend to the main street near the post office.

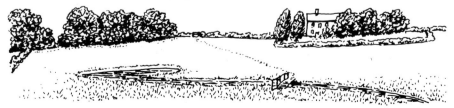

30

The BISLEY - BOURNES GREEN Walk

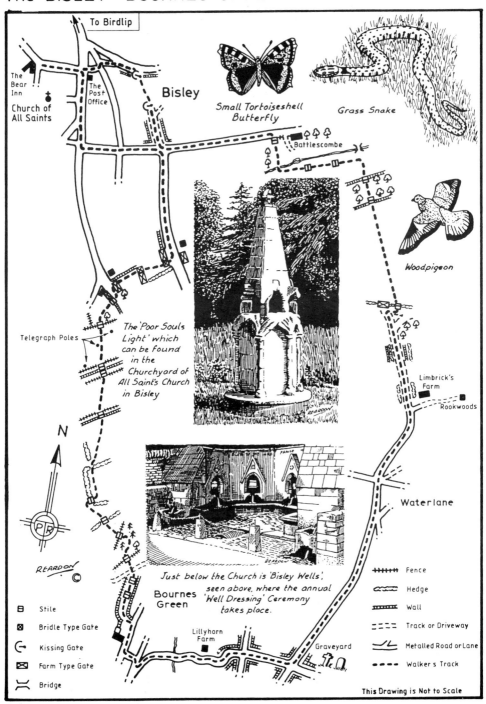

To Birdlip

The Bear Inn

Church of All Saints

The Post Office

Bisley

Small Tortoiseshell Butterfly

Grass Snake

Battlescombe

Woodpigeon

Telegraph Poles

The 'Poor Souls Light' which can be found in the Churchyard of All Saint's Church in Bisley

Limbrick's Farm

Rookwoods

N

Waterlane

REARDON ©

Just below the Church is 'Bisley Wells', seen above, where the annual 'Well Dressing' Ceremony takes place.

Bournes Green

Lillyhorn Farm

Graveyard

⊟	Stile
⊠	Bridle Type Gate
⊂	Kissing Gate
⊠	Farm Type Gate
⋋	Bridge

┼┼┼┼	Fence
∿∿	Hedge
▥▥▥	Wall
= = =	Track or Driveway
⌐⌐	Metalled Road or Lane
● ● ●	Walker's Track

This Drawing is Not to Scale

8 Barnsley-Ampney Crucis

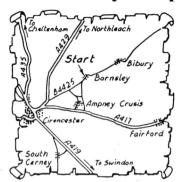

Distance: 5 miles.
Time: 2¼ hours of continuous walking.
Map: OS Pathfinder 1114 (SP00/10 Cirencester).
Starting Point: Grid ref 077051
Terrain: Almost completely flat. The paths for the most part take you over fields and on tracks.
Refreshments: The Village Inn in Barnsley and the Butcher's Arms at Ampney Crucis.

Here we venture to a part of the Cotswolds sometimes rather neglected by walkers. This is a pity because, although the scenery is less dramatic than elsewhere in the area, it has a character all of its own and is notable particularly for its tranquillity.

Park with care where you can in the vicinity of the Village Inn which is at the centre of the village of Barnsley. Although Barnsley is run through by a fairly busy road, this does not detract too much from its appeal, composed as it is of cottages in the darker-hued stone of the southern Cotswolds and watched over by the interesting-looking church, largely Norman, although only completed in the 17th century. Worthy of note is the Norman window in the organ chamber.

Turn right from the pub and cross the road onto a pavement. Continue along here for a while, passing several houses, and a road on the left (which leads up to a barn and a proper red telephone box), until, opposite a discreet sign on the other side of the road where it begins to curve away, you come to a track on the left which runs beside the stone wall of Barnsley House. Walk up here, catching glimpses of the gardens on the right with their sloping lawns and rows of rollmop bushes, as well as the modest lines of the house itself and the imposing church tower away to the left. The path will take you through the nursery and past the car park on the left and the entrance to the house on the right. Pass through a gate and at the end of the stone wall you will meet a junction of tracks at a farm, with a goodly selection of sheds, where you turn right.

The high stone wall turns right with you, tree branches leaning over it to grasp you, with a nursery garden on your left. Pass a gate into the statuesque back garden of the house on the right, which look very enticing, and tennis courts, as fields appear ahead of you. As the walls drop away, a clipped hedge takes its place on the right, with an unclipped hedge to the left, and the countryside opens up.

Head towards a gate into a field. Pass through and hug the hedge on the left beyond a ditch. On the other side there is a field containing circular structures that in design resemble more than somewhat the tents of the nomads of the Mongolian steppe. Desolated woodland then appears on the left until you come to a double stile.

Once you have negotiated these you will find yourself in a marshy meadow, green suffused with a briny yellow. Stretch out across it diagonally right in the general direction of a cottage, next to which is a wind pump which, on closer inspection, is arthritic with rust. By the cottage pass over a stile (if necessary), turn right onto a metalled track and almost immediately turn left across a stile into a field and head for the woods, Barnsley having all but disappeared behind you.

Ahead now are the woods. Head for a corner of them in front of you and pass to the left of a crumbling perimeter wall in the direction of an abutment of woodland. Away to the left are regularly enclosed fields and in their midst, a few farm buildings. Where the two areas of woodland meet, a stile leads straight ahead onto a green track. The woods on the right give way to a wide clearing whilst the woods to the left have a swampy look.

Ignore any other paths until the track sweeps away to the right at the end of the clearing. Don't follow this but go straight ahead into a field with woodland on your right. Keep to the right hand margin of the field and continue to the end of the wall at a gateway, quite possibly barred by a large log.

Leap over this to find yourself at a roadside. Turn right here, passing a cottage on the left and another logged entrance to the woods on the right. Soon you will come to a junction, with Barnsley marked to the right, and to the left, the direction you require: the Ampneys and Poulton. It is a quiet though open country lane running between hedges and fields, the example to your right planted with young saplings. As you proceed there are glimpses of buildings ahead of you to the right and, directly ahead, a metal Dutch barn. Before the barn there is some very prettily-clipped hedge on the right, sloping in a cascade.

A footpath sign appears on the right which you ignore; but as you draw alongside the barn on the left, swaying like a moribund spider, there is another footpath on the right, leading into a field. Enter the field and bear half left across it, more or less in the direction of some houses you can see in the far corner. At a certain point, before long, you will meet the imprint of tractor wheels and it might be easier to follow these to the left hand margin and then turn right until you come to the stone stile on your left which is to be found in the vicinity of a footpath sign poking up from beyond the hedge. The stile is inserted between the second and third big trees from the right.

Cross the stile onto a track and then immediately over another stile into a field. Go directly ahead in the general direction of some houses you see to the left of a little gathering of fir trees. At the corner pass through a gateway between houses and head for the road. This is the beginning of Ampney Crucis, which has a splendid church and within its churchyard a rare and beautiful 14th century cross. To visit the church turn right and follow the road as it bears left. The Butcher's Arms can also be found by turning right and then second right.

For the walk, turn left and walk along the pavement through the village, passing a graveyard on the right dominated by a small half-timbered shed which contains wheelbarrows and the like. Not long after you pass an invisible frontier into the older part of the village where the road is flanked by stone cottages surrounded by flowers and bushes. The road passes a pillar box and curves down to a junction where you turn left.

Pass the entrance to Dudley Farm on the right and then opposite some massive hedges on the left there is a path over a stile into a field. Bear half left across the field following a diagonal line in the direction of a house at a corner. To the right, as you walk, there are extensive views with a farm largely composed of grey corrugated buildings beyond which is a very upright building like a doll's house.

As you approach the house at the corner, another house, until now well concealed behind trees, will appear to the left. Between the two you will find a stone stile which will take you onto a lane. Go straight ahead, sauntering past Hilcot House, follow the road around to the left until you see a vision in pink before you. Turn right in front of this house and head down a narrow defile between a garage on the left and a house on the right. This will bring you to a stile beyond which is a field. Cross the field more or less directly, angling slightly to the left, until another stile arises. Go over this into another meadow, one of those decorated with a single tree.

Turn left and, keeping close to the left-hand margin, wade through the grass until you come to a gate. Pass through into another field, complete with two trees and continue through a double hunting gate into another field, this one also with two trees. At the end of this field, as you approach a farm on the right, there is a wall but in the corner on the left is a gate which will take you across a bridge into a neighbouring field where you turn right. Go forward and at the corner pass into the next field, where the little brook is your companion on your right. A stile in the corner will take you into another field and the suburbs of Barnsley reappear before you. Away to the left is the woodland alongside which you walked earlier.

At the corner of this field a gate and a bridge will take you to a stile beyond which is a lane, the former Roman Akeman Street. Cross this, turn right and then immediately left to pass through a metal gate into a field. Continue forward with a hedge on the right, whilst a strange burrow on the left cuts into the field for a short distance, as if made by a mole with ambition. As you walk, the cottage by the windpump will reappear ahead of you to the left.

Then you will pass a disused quarry, now a pond, just to the left, after which you will come to a stile. Cross this, with a large house in front of you, and then turn immediately left, heading towards a stile. This will take you over a bridge and then another stile. After this turn immediately right alongside a hedge, then woodland, cross the metalled lane you encountered earlier and follow the margin of the field until you come to a familiar pair of stiles. Cross these, continue forward to the gates at the other end of the field and retrace your steps past Barnsley House but instead of turning left through the nursery carry on and bear left through the farm. This track will bring you back into the heart of the village.

The 'Village Pub' in the
village of Barnsley

The BARNSLEY - AMPNEY CRUCIS Walk

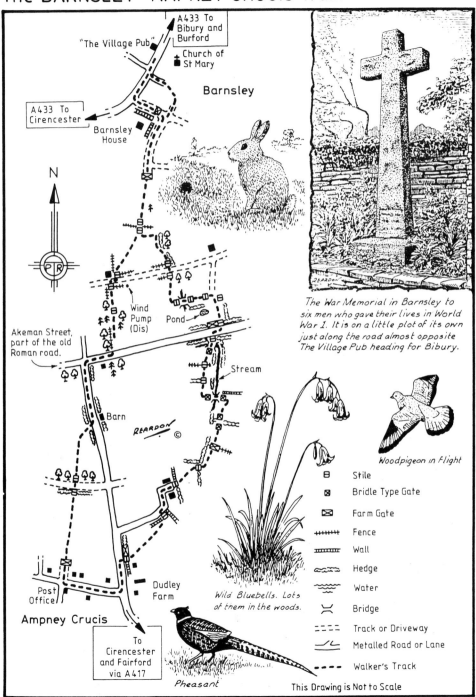

A433 To Bibury and Burford

"The Village Pub"

Church of St Mary

Barnsley

A433 To Cirencester

Barnsley House

N

Wind Pump (Dis)

Pond

Akeman Street, part of the old Roman road.

Stream

Barn

REARDON ©

Woodpigeon in Flight

Stile

Bridle Type Gate

Farm Gate

Fence

Wall

Hedge

Water

Bridge

Track or Driveway

Metalled Road or Lane

Walker's Track

Post Office

Dudley Farm

Ampney Crucis

To Cirencester and Fairford via A417

Wild Bluebells. Lots of them in the woods.

Pheasant

This Drawing is Not to Scale

The War Memorial in Barnsley to six men who gave their lives in World War 1. It is on a little plot of its own just along the road almost opposite The Village Pub heading for Bibury.

9 Chipping Campden-Broad Campden

Distance: 5 miles
Time: 2 hours of uninterrupted walking
Map: OS Pathfinder 1043 (Broadway and Chipping Campden, SP 03/13)
Starting Point: Grid ref 135399
Terrain: Fields among which only one should be unpleasantly muddy. Not too many climbs, either.
Refreshments: Any number of hostelries in Chipping Campden and the Baker's Arms at Broad Campden

This walk can present a basic problem: how to avoid the mud which is seemingly ever-present after even the merest hint of rain. Of course, it cannot be done, except in the driest of summer months, but the following route should prove a successful compromise whatever the recent weather.

Start from the National Trust car park on Dover's Hill, just off Kingcomb Lane, a little to the north west of the village. Turn left out of the car park and walk back down to Kingcomb Lane (you will have the opportunity to enjoy the views, tantalising glimpses of which can be caught now and at the end of the walk).

Cross Kingcomb Lane and walk down Dyer's Lane in the direction of Chipping Campden. On the left is a row of trees whose trunks are cloaked in green. Below, a thatched cottage will appear. As you approach it, cross to the left-hand side of the road where there is a skeletal pavement. Pass another cottage on the left and then turn left along a footpath which will take you into a field.

Once in the field, bear right across it in the direction of houses at the edge of Chipping Campden, with the distinctive splendour of its church away to the left. The path is quite likely to be fairly obvious, a long weal of brown mud, which will bring you to the edge of the town. Go through onto a path which will lead past houses to a road; cross this to continue along a path, ignoring a footpath on the left, posted for Dover's Hill until you come to another road.

Turn right here, passing cottages with handsome iron canopies on the right, a recently consecrated burial ground on the left, and then, on the left, at the junction with the High Street, St Catherine's Catholic Church.

Cross over here and turn to the left, to gaze on one of the fairest streets in Europe, a long, curving road flanked by houses and shops of all shapes and sizes, each running headlong into the next – a magnificent jumble of ochre stone and tumbling chimneys.

Chipping Campden was at its most prosperous during the late Middle Ages when Cotswold wool was cherished throughout Europe. When the centre of the wool trade shifted to the continent, Campden did not adapt well to the weaving industry that took its place, due to an absence of water, and thus preserved a measure of tranquillity still evident in comparison with some other of the showpiece Cotswold towns.

As an old guidebook asks: "*Whence came this intense feeling for the traditions and styles of building in the Cotswolds?"*

In 1902 the William Morris Guild of Handicrafts arrived here which might explain the large number of jewellery and handicraft shops. Continue along the High Street until just before the Post Office, where you turn right through an arch into the courtyard of the Noel Arms. Continue between some newly-built cottages until you come to a road.

Continue straight on as the road crosses a stream, rises, leaving a nice view of Campden roofs behind you and narrows to a path which will eventually pass a low wall on the right beyond which are playing fields. The path takes you through a gate and then widens before continuing to a road. Immediately on the left a tarmac track leads into a field.

Enter this and turn directly right along a path with a hedge to the right running parallel with the road. At a point where the hedge ends by a house with some nice topiary in its garden, the road veers away to the right. Your path, however, dips and rises up a bank to cross a sunken stream. Not long after, the path will diverge at a post and stone slab, bear right, with the remains of a stone wall on the left, towards a house.

Ignore another path on the left, pass through a kissing gate and, keeping to the right of the house, approach a driveway and cut across it between a pair of staddle stones to a gate tucked in at the corner of a house and stone wall. Pass through and follow the path around as it passes between the low cottages of Broad Campden and then, on the left, the Quaker Friends' Meeting House, a simple building dating back to 1663.

It is associated with a certain Jonathon Hulls, a far-sighted 18th century clock repairer who invented the slide-rule but whose attempt to propel a boat by steam ended in ignominious failure.

You will emerge on the green, with its conveniently located bench opposite a Victorian church with eccentric tower. Pass the church and, at the road, turn left past a sign which indicates that the road is unsuitable for motors. Descend, with a brook bubbling across a meadow to your right, to a corner and follow the road as it rises towards a cottage set up high on the left and substantial wall on the right. Immediately after the cottage as the houses of Broad Campden appear before you, is a gateway on the left.

Go through here and head towards a gate, pass through a paddock, with a shed to the left, to another gate. Once through the gate you are in an orchard. Head left down an obvious path alongside a hedge. Pass a stile on the right and continue to another stile and a stone bridge, with an ornamental garden on the left. Once over the bridge, turn immediately right along the bottom edge of a field, with the brook gurgling at your side beyond a hedge.

Campden church will loom over the brow of a hill and, after a while, you will come to a point at the corner of the field where the brook streams away to the right and a gap appears in the hedge before you which crosses another stream and leads into the next field. Pass through and continue directly across another gap into another field which lies slightly askew, tilted leftwards. By bearing slightly left across this field, more or less in line with the hedge to your left, you will come to a stile. Once over the stile bear left again, keeping to the right of two sentinel trees in the middle of the field.

A perfect view of the church, looking like a cardboard cut-out for a model railway, surrounded by ornamental evergreens, arises, with all the roofs of Chipping Campden arrayed to the left. The path will bring you to a tangled, seemingly dried-up pond, certainly a haven for birds. Bear left and follow the curve of the bushes to the right, and cross a stile into a field. Cross the field to another stream, the River Cam, and follow it left towards Chipping Campden once again. You will pass two bridges on the right, a stone arch – presumably part of the church estate at one time – and then come to a gate on the right, just before a solid wooden fence. Go through the gate to follow a path which crosses the river and then, after a stile, bears sharp left to a drive.

Turn right again and follow the road as it curves up to the left and eventually arrives at Church Street, by twin thatched cottages. The church, most definitely worth a visit, is to the right. Turn left and follow the road past the Eight Bells until you meet the High Street. Just before the junction you will pass Perry's Cottage on the left, a name which figured in a bizarre episode known as the Campden Wonder.

In 1660 one William Harrison, the 70-year-old steward of Lady Juliana Hicks, disappeared, with only his bloodstained comb and neckerchief coming to light. His servant, John Perry, was hanged for the crime on nearby Fish Hill, along with his mother and brother. Two years later, Harrison showed up, spinning a yarn involving kidnap, Turkish pirates, slavery and who knows what else. His wife subsequently committed suicide and the judiciary refused to acknowledge his return.

Cross the street and turn left. Once again you may savour the glory of this street, passing on this occasion the old covered market. Carry on until you come to the Catholic church again and turn right to retrace your steps as far as a thatched cottage at a corner where the road bears right. Turn left up a residential road with the thatched cottage on your left. Soon enough, this road will become a track and then a path which, as you pass a farm on the left, is fenced off from the main track. Follow this up, with, perhaps, glimpses of Broadway Tower to the left, to where it meets the main road, Kingcomb Lane.

Turn left for a few yards until you see a signpost pointing across the road to a path which follows the right hand margin of a field. Follow this until you come to a stile beneath trees at a corner. On the other side is Dover's Hill. Over the stile and turn left, picking your way back to the car park.

But of course you must wander to the lip of the hill for one of the mightiest views in Christendom, across the plain, the Vale of Evesham, to far distant hills. The hill is named after Robert Dover, a local lawyer who in the early 17th century created the Cotswold 'Olympick' games here, which were famous across the land. Events, including staff-fighting and shin-kicking, were not for the faint-hearted; and by the 19th century the unruliness of contestants, and spectators, led to the outlawing of the games.

In recent years, however, they have been revived, taking place on the eve of Scuttlebrook Wake, a local festival which takes place on the Saturday before the Spring Holiday.

The CHIPPING CAMPDEN - BROAD CAMPDEN Walk

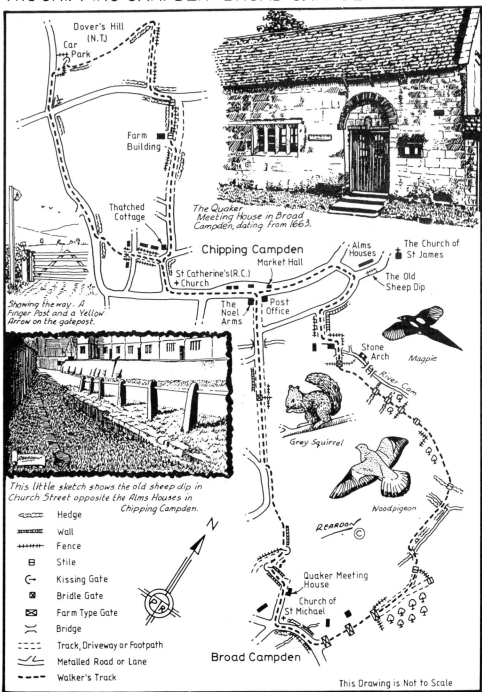

Dover's Hill (N.T.)
Car Park

Farm Building

Thatched Cottage

The Quaker Meeting House in Broad Campden, dating from 1663.

Showing the way. A Finger Post and a Yellow Arrow on the gatepost.

Chipping Campden
Market Hall
St Catherine's (R.C.) + Church
The Noel Arms
Post Office

Alms Houses
The Church of St James
The Old Sheep Dip

Stone Arch
River Cam
Magpie

Grey Squirrel

Woodpigeon

REARDON ©

Quaker Meeting House
Church of St Michael

Broad Campden

This little sketch shows the old sheep dip in Church Street opposite the Alms Houses in Chipping Campden.

〜〜〜	Hedge
〓〓〓	Wall
+++++	Fence
日	Stile
┌	Kissing Gate
⊠	Bridle Gate
⊠	Farm Type Gate
⤙	Bridge
- - - -	Track, Driveway or Footpath
〜ㄴ	Metalled Road or Lane
▬ ▬ ▬	Walker's Track

N

This Drawing is Not to Scale

39

10 Cold Aston-Notgrove-Turkdean

Distance: 5 miles
Time: 2 hours
Map: OS Pathfinder 1067 (SP 02/12, Stow-on-the-Wold)   and   OS Pathfinder 1090 (SP01/11 Northleach and Andoversford).
Starting Point: Grid ref 129198
Terrain: A substantial amount of road walking but on lanes with little traffic. Some woodland path and meadow.
Refreshments: The Plough Inn at Cold Aston

This walk takes you on top of the wold. An uncomplicated, though longer, stroll which takes you through three typical, tranquil and unspoilt upland villages set in open countryside.

Park with care in the village of Cold Aston and locate the Plough Inn. Cold Aston was originally just Aston. It became Cold Aston in the 13th century and then Aston Blank in the 16th and, today, seems to be known by both names. The church, its Celtic origins indicated by the lack of east window, also boasts a fine and massive yew.

Turn left out of the pub and walk along the road in the direction of Notgrove. The green with its spreading sycamore tree and proper red telephone box is agreeably quiet and the road will take you away from it past a succession of tall stone cottages. The road will curve left, with the Church of England school on the right, and pass a cluster of houses which seem to be built around a farmyard on the left.

Then the village peters out to pass a narrow lane on the left marked by a No Through Road sign, and the countryside opens up across the fields on either side of you in shallow undulations, marked with the tracery of weathered dry stone walling. Here you are on top of the Wold.

Away to the right vehicles slice silently through a distant road and, although the land is clearly fertile farming country, it bears that empty, barely-inhabited look. The road bends around a little to the right towards a row of houses and passes them. Soon after you will notice a great avenue of trees slanting away to the left. As you approach them you will not fail to remark a gate just before them and beside it a bridle gate.

Go through this to bear right onto a path which will take you along this long perspective of beeches with their very straight trunks and precise heights, giving a slightly unnerving perfection to these green and brown surroundings. Underfoot may be muddy in patches, pounded by hooves.

At the end of the first part you will come to a gate. Kink slightly right, then left and continue straight through another slender plantation as the roofs of Notgrove and a farm tower appear to the right. Towards the end you will pass some low horse jumps (if they remain) and come to a gate which leads to a farmyard track.

40

PICTURESQUE COTTAGES IN A SECLUDED CORNER of COLD ASTON in GLOUCESTERSHIRE — REARDON

Turn right along the track, on the far side of which is a mossy wall and plantation until very soon, where the wall seems to arch into a hump, you come to a gate on the left. Pass through this into a wide, sloping field, with the attractive houses of Notgrove, and its church, spread around about it like a model village. Head on down the meadow, dotted with enclosed trees, which is one of those that makes you want to spread your arms and glide down it, and head on up to the far side where there is a gate about 100 yards to the right of the church, with its ice-cream cone spire. The church bears a Saxon crucifix on its exterior east wall whilst within is a monument to the Whittington family, of Lord Mayor of London and pantomime fame.

Once through the gate turn left to visit the church, if you so desire, whilst the walk continues by turning right and taking the road which, having wound up here from below in a hairpin, continues to wander through the village passing to the right of a barn with a dovecote at the apex of its roof. The narrow road curls to the left passing stables to the right, and a spiky, anaemic fir tree, and then the entrance to the manor on the left, with its avenue of neatly emasculated trees leading down to the church.

Continue along this road, ignoring a road leading away to the right, and noticing beyond a wall to the left, in an ancient partition, a well-turned window. Eventually you will come to a junction where you turn left in the direction of Turkdean along a road which is unlikely to carry much traffic to speak of. There are extensive views away to the right, large fields mostly, dotted with farmhouses and covered with patches of woodland. There seems to be little colour but as you walk the browns and greens spread into different shades, particularly in the early spring light.

To the left, beyond a stone wall, is a meadow and a gateway. Further on there is another entrance to the manor by a lodge, with a pair of handsome gates with a gilded crest. Then to the left appears a pair of windowless sheds. To the right another avenue of trees accompanies the route in stately procession but you are to stay on the road for the time being. Soon the trees are left behind and the road climbs very gently, passing a farm embedded in a bottom to the left and sheltered by trees.

Pass a track to the right leading down to an old stone barn as the road straightens up towards the brow. The panorama has subtly changed by now and somehow presents a warmer aspect – to the right the far undulations rollercoaster against the straight near horizon formed by the fields. And then, just after a building on the right that has somehow found itself up to the neck in field, the land corkscrews into a vortex, after which, just as the road bears right and begins to descend, you will spy Turkdean church tower. For the first time in an age you can see real hills in the far distance.

As you enter this soundless village yet another avenue of trees appears on the left and then, opposite a farm with its stone barns, a little green and a notice with No Through Road written on it.

Of Turkdean H.J. Massingham said (in Wold Without End): *"In the churchyard, where violets are white, the wayfarer is on a level with these roofs whose abutments and slantings compose so treasured a mental etching"*.

Turn left here by the sign down a track, passing a very attractive mullion-windowed house and courtyard on the right and descend back into the countryside which seems to have attracted a number of colourful, warbling birds.

The track rises with woodland on the right before levelling out and dropping again as the houses of Cold Aston reappear before you on the far side of the valley. To their left the beech avenue is discernible. The track curls through the valley bottom, one side of which is like a rough cheese with its rind pared from it. Then the road rises steeply through a gateway. To the left you will notice a noisy rookery and then the track will begin to level out. Eventually you will pass a couple of new houses on the left, the stoniness of the ground very much in evidence; and soon the path will emerge in the heart of Cold Aston, at which point you turn right for the pub.

NOTGROVE, AN UNSPOILT VILLAGE NESTLING IN THE COTSWOLD HILLS of GLOUCESTERSHIRE.

The COLD ASTON-NOTGROVE-TURKDEAN Walk

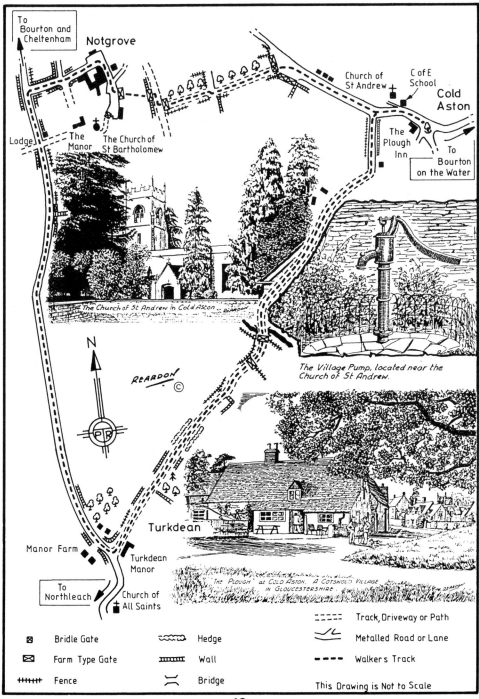

To Bourton and Cheltenham

Notgrove

Church of St Andrew

C of E School

Cold Aston

The Plough Inn

To Bourton on the Water

Lodge

The Manor

The Church of St Bartholomew

The Church of St Andrew in Cold Aston.

The Village Pump, located near the Church of St Andrew.

REARDON ©

N

Turkdean

Manor Farm

Turkdean Manor

To Northleach

Church of All Saints

"THE PLOUGH" at COLD ASTON. A COTSWOLD VILLAGE IN GLOUCESTERSHIRE.

⊠ Bridle Gate	᷇᷇᷇ Hedge	⎓⎓⎓ Track, Driveway or Path
⊠ Farm Type Gate	⊞⊞⊞ Wall	Metalled Road or Lane
+++++ Fence	⊰ Bridge	- - - Walkers Track

This Drawing is Not to Scale

43

REARDON PUBLISHING

A family run publishing house based in Cheltenham, producing guides to the Cotswold area, using local authors, and having the books printed in the Gloucestershire Cotswolds.

Other books in the Walkabout series

Cotswold Walkabout (book one)
Cotswold Walkabout (book two)
Cotswold Hillwalks
Cotswold Riverwalks
The Cotswold Way
The Donnington Way
The Echo's Cotswold Walks
The Echo's Second book of Cotswold Walks
The Echo's Third book of Cotswold Walks
Gloucestershire and Forest of Dean Walks (book one)
Gloucestershire and Forest of Dean Walks (book two)
Walks around Burford
Walks around Chipping Norton
Walks around Gt Tew and the Rollright Stones
Walks around the Slaughters
Walks around Stow on the Wold

Please send a S.A.E. for our free Booklist and Orderform
To: **REARDON PUBLISHING, 56, UPPER NORWOOD STREET, LECKHAMPTON, CHELTENHAM, GLOS. GL53 0DU**